T0195940

VERMILLION CITY

A selection of poems

GEORGE A. COX

authorHOUSE®

AuthorHouse™ UK
1663 Liberty Drive
Bloomington, IN 47403 USA
www.authorhouse.co.uk
Phone: 0800 047 8203 (Domestic TFN)
*   +44 1908 723714 (International)*

Published by AuthorHouse 05/23/2019

ISBN: 978-1-7283-8871-7 (sc)
ISBN: 978-1-7283-8872-4 (e)

Print information available on the last page.

Any people depicted in stock imagery provided by Getty Images are models, and such images are being used for illustrative purposes only.
Certain stock imagery © Getty Images.

This book is printed on acid-free paper.

CONTENTS

PANORAMA

From atop a lone high rock
I watched the ocean
Smashing beneath me
In cascades of jumbled green

White horses play hide and seek
In the hills and valleys
Of endless changing
Panorama

We are born of her womb
Whose tides surge through our veins
Would destroy our own mother

THE PILL

I took my pill this morning
It made me feel quite ill
So to the doctor I trotted
He gave me another pill

The black one tasted lovely
The white one bitter sweet
The blue one for water retention
And to keep my figure neat

A purple pill for when I laugh
A yellow when I frown
A stripey pill for inbetween
And on occasion there's a brown

Valium for my emotions
Aspirin for my head
Lithium for mood swings
Temazepam for bed

I took my pill this evening
It made me feel quite ill
It's a common reaction the doctor said
So take another pill

HOMONID

At first I walked
On four legs
Now on two
My eyes point forward
Like gunsights of the mind
Flame is my ally
My slave, my keeper

Now
Crystal fingers
Of laser light
Do my bidding
I am Man, Sapient
TheWise

Vermillion City

Down vermillion streets full of twisted signs
'Cross pavements cracked with a thousand lines
I wander hopeless and in dread
In this unreal city of the dead

As I wander this lonely city
Full of pain, devoid of pity
One vermillion thought comes to mind
To follow the street of twisted signs

Where it will lead no one knows
To a door open or one closed
Down vermillion streets full of twisted signs
'Cross pavements cracked with a thousand lines.

LOGIC MINUS

Man quests in a maze
There is logic in his questing
But no sense of yin or yang
In the maze are an infinity
Of exits, but only one leads

To Godhead

From the oceans, deep and cold
To the reefs of space
And out beyond the system
With probing fingers of
Twenty one centimetre hydrogen

UnlockingGod

God watches his children racing
Like rats in a grandiose maze
And in the watching, it is good

And when our children, run the maze
Will we like HIM laugh
with thinVICIOUS humour

MANTIS

Preying mantis gantries
Hang in girdered silence
Groping down toward their prey
Bales-Bundles-Cartons

With slow precise movements
They stab them
With hooks of iron

And lift effortless
Into the sky

The open holds of the squat
Beetlelike barges
Wait
In water lapped quiet
For their cold hard touch

The predator and the prey
Linked
By lines of hardest steel

GROUND ZERO

A new sun awoke that day
Delivered, express, by Enola Gay
Children playing with a ball
Enthroned forever on the wall

Innocence ended at Hiroshima

TELEPHONE

From afar your message comes
Heralded, by trilling bell
Clamouring din
For some just a voice
For others Samaritan lifeline
Lovers whisper endearments
And wish they could run
The high strung wires
To electric embrace

T.V. Sits like haunted fishtank
One – way cylcopean eye
Full of electronic ghosts
Mass communication surrounds us
But only the telephone
Lets us talk from afar

Pharoahs Of Mars

Across a plain of crystal red sand
A thin cold wind blows forever restless
Stirring in its thinness a few lifeless dunes
At the poles of this strange red planet
Small fields of lifeless frost
Lie close to the ground in intimate embrace

Close to the plain of Tethys, lies a great canyon
Forever it seems to run in mighty rifts
On the left bank, toward the middle of the rift
Stand two mighty pyramids towering toward the sky
Sentinal like in the thin cold air
Did some lifeform build these huge monoliths
Or are they a strange fluke of nature
Did once the waves of a mighty river
Lap at these monuments to unreal Pharoahs

TEARS

Nor all thy crystal tinted tears
Will wash away the rough lined years
Nor all thy heart nor mind
Wear away the years so blind

When all is said and done
This life is but an endless run
Down the canyons of the mind
Toward you destiny to unwind

The end is marked in DEATHS own print
And no one beats the REAPERS stint
So fill a glass and supp with me
Together we'll fulfill our destiny

But DEATH is not an ending
Of this you should be sure
The REAPER is not the enemy
He just opens another door.

THE PEDLAR

Pedlar comes over bright morning vale
Pedalling his wares over heathery dale
Wandering his long lonely trudging way
Sleeping by night and travelling by day

All tied about with pots and pans
Skinny of rib and loose of hands
People coming from miles around
To see the pedlar on his round

Bright of eye, face all tanned
This then is the pedlar man
Glinting in the morning sun
Waiting for the childrens run

Knife to sharpen, axe to mend
Pots to sell and tale to send
Walking across the evening vale
To sleep upon the heathery dale

DOWNBOUND EXPRESS

I am waiting on a lonely station
Just an empty tomb
The downbound express is my destination
There's no telling where i'm bound

INDEED

The snake and the chimpanzee
were arguing
the snake lost
and
walked away
in disgust
the chimpanzee
slithered
to his tree
a very strange argument
indeed

HIVE

Bees scurry
Hither and tither
Tuned to the hive
Antenna searching
Heaven-ward
SeekingGOD

Bi-Polar

Across convoluted fields of grey
Streaking through ego and id
Time seems heavy, seconds eternity
Reason explodes toward chaos
Unreal clouds fog my mind
Strange thoughts beckon to me
I know I am trapped
In this biological hell
Cycle upon cycle of unreason
Down to the shores
Of a bizarre ocean
But this I know
Should I ever wade
To the depths
Of this surreal sea
MANIC IMPLOSION

HOUSE

She sits, lonely, unwanted, unloved
The skirts of her gardens now untouched
Where children frolicked to the
Happy sounds of ball on bat
Here limbered thighs flashed
As raqueted ball flew to and fro
And now to her just a memory
All that remains now are jumbled bushes
The amber flash of cruising bees
Skipping flight of careless butterflies
Chirping multi-colour birds
Hoping, oneday, someday, soon;

And inside her red and dusty walls
Where lovers played games of exploration
And many a glass was supped and filled
And children played as children do
And now to her just a memory
Now only spiders court and dance
The windows of her eyes, the doors of her face
Are they blank, staring, open to the world
Or do they somehow look inward
Hoping, oneday, someday, soon

CRANES

The cranes leave their nests
in the marshes

Their wings cast soft crimson
shadows on the reeds

Slow quiet wingbeats fill
the air with peace

They glide white and pure
in the dawn sun

Simple fisher-folk in the marshes, give thanks
for the luck they will bring
At the end of the day
the cranes return

Wings glowing soft crimson
in the setting sun

THE OTHER MARTIAN CHRONICLES

Next to the sea a new sun awakes
Man hurls his needle upward
At it's tip Mariner swims in an endless sea
It's destination that strange red planet
No mans foot will step on this alien soil
There will be no giant leap forward
Only the machineries of man this time
An on reaching Mars, the message comes
There is no life nor has there been
And after a time the batteries die
The probe lies still and quiet
And if only the cameras could see
The strange figure on his six-legged mount
And when mans foot sets down
On the distant shores of the red planet
Will DejahThoris, Princess of Mars
With regal grace dain to meet us

FUTILITY

Across a Somme battlefield barren and grey
Very flares reach upto the cloud filled sky
Then flicker and die like discarded stars
As through thrown to the heavens
By an angry petulant child
Flags, hang, damply, in the still misty dawn
DEATH laughs with infinite patience from the wings

Through the wire the enemy are sighted
Jumping and leaping as the bullets hit them
The two sides converge and meet in the trenches
In a welter of grenades and bayonets
Which corner of a foreign field for the dead
Only the reaper laughs from the wings

Many miles to the rear the generals sit and drink port
And with each sip, how many more soldiers
Will join their comrades on the wire?

ALONE

You ask me, why I sit here alone?
There is none here to comfort me

You ask me, if I am unwell in spirit?
If I am alone and afraid then it must be so

You ask me, if I want your company?
It is yours to give or not

You ask me, will I take your hand?
How can I when I don't know the price

You ask me, to reach out to you in trust?
I would but I fear rejection

And you say to me, How can I reject when I as you suffer.

LOBOTOMY SOUP

My brain is gone through
The hole in my head
There is no more madness
No more dread

But why did they? Take away
My brain
For Lobotomy soup

All the pretty madness
All the pretty sadness
All the things said
All the things done

Now I am one
Now I am gone

TALES

Sunlight glimmers on the still clear pool
Ripples mark the passage of cruising fish
And if they could talk, what tales they'd tell.

Dragonfly hovers, crystalline wings beating
The air to a shimmering haze
And if it could talk, what tales it would tell.

The kingfisher sits on his lonely perch
In glistening rainbow colours, scanning for
supper
And if it could talk, what tales it would tell.

Sitting by the water's edge is a young man
It is I, and if you come closer and listen
What tales I will tell.

BLOODHYPE

Down through the ages in endless spite
Bursting across the centuries in an endless rite
Must this Bloodhype go on and on
Have we to write destructions tome

From Cro-magnon man with naked axe
To modern man with nuclear pax
Must this Bloodhype go on and on
Will we write destructions tome

Across the third world's savagery
Borders all the worlds lunacy
Must this Bloodhype go on and on
Why must we write destructions tome

The end of the world is drawing near
The reasons are so boundless clear
Must this Bloodhype go on and on
Let's try to end destructions tome

SATAN'S HAMMER

Comet, comet flashing bright
Like a hammer in the night
Spreading as a celestial fan
Catch us, catch us if you can

In she comes with curving grace
About to start the deadly race
Across the planets burning bright
Like a hammer in the night

Into the maelstrom gaining speed
Burning like a demon steed
On she comes heading nearer
Dreadful tidings Baleful bearer

And on to Earth home of man
Is this the end ofGods great plan
The comet misses, the vagerants past
The home of man is safe at last

Out of the system with curving grace
Away from the planets the end of the race
She is harmless burning bright
Like a hammer in the night

She will wait for her orbit to bend
So that she can visit again
Down toward the sun so bright
Like a hammer in the night

TELEVISION

Lovers kiss
symbolically
Cars race in
endless
dyaramas
Flesh explodes
in gruesome
reality
Detectives find
the murderer
And all of this
from the
comfort
Of your own
armchair
On the box.

INTELLIGENCE

What terrible talent
Enthrones our minds
Like a two edged sword
At our hearts

This democlian gift
Given by god
That sows our souls
With dark, with light

IDITAROD TRAIL

Across the savage wilderness
Travelling nose to tail
Man and pack together
On the Iditarod trail

So mush you handsome doggies
You ain't tired yet
There's another twenty miles to go
Before the sun is set

A thousand miles of frozen hell
Before the race is run
Nine more days of loneliness
Before it's lost or won

So mush you handsome doggies
You ain't tired yet
Just one more hill to climb
Before the sun is set

Nine loyal husky's on the trace
Always on the go
Lead dog, Sampson, pulling hard
Loping through the snow

So mush you handsome doggies
You ain't tired yet
Cross one more frozen river
Before the sun is set

One more day of ice and wind
One more day to run
One more day on the frozen trail
Before the race is won

Travelling Man

Out along the shore where
The tumbling breakers crash
All along the cliffs where
The raging combers smash

Underneath the city where
The sun will never show
Down in the sewers where
All the dead things go

"SAYINGS"

"Your never alone with schizophrenia",
"Don't drink and drive, smoke dope and fly",
"If it ain't fu*ked, don't fix it",
"I'm not superstitiuous, touch wood!",
"I'd give my right arm, to be ambidextrous!",
"Fight for peace, is like fu*king for virginity!",
"Be alert, Britain needs lerts!",
"I like E.C.T., but it goes right to my head!",
"Heroin is moorish",
"One world, one people, maybe",
"Your not paranoid, They are really after you!",
"Woodstock, sex, drugs and rock' and 'roll",
"If you go down to the woods today, be it on your own head!",
"To ask a question, you must already know part of the answer!",
"You've never felt that kind of pain, till you've felt that kind of love!",
"Join the army, meet exotic new people and kill them!",
"Life sucks and then you die!"
"To understand all is to forgive all",
"Forgive your enemies, it annoys them!".

UNDER THE SHADOW

Under the shadow
Of the bomb
Mass destruction
Welcomes us
With open arms
Unfurls with techno-fury
MEGA DEATH

LOVE

She is my lover
She is my wife
She is my comforter
She is my torment

My sullen hatred
For her
Spills out
In tears of joy

CLOUDS

The clouds drift by
Dressed in somber grey
Defying man's futile borders
Untouched by our longing
Unmindful of our anguish

Homonids reach out
From deep, dark depths
To the reefs of space
Far beyond the system
Searching for god

Man with his glowing sword
Of nuclear power
Can light our humble lives
Or in a moment of blind panic
Destroy us

TIME-WINDS

The timewinds blow
Over shattered reality
Wrenching at our souls
In the evening of our lives

Smack-Head

The candle stutters
In incandescent fire
Crisping the foil

The fumes rise
Rotating through air
Bringing forth pleasure

I kiss the dragons breath
She is wishin me
Pulsating-Sensual-Sentinient

I dream dragon dreams
In magical landscapes
All in silent majesty

Then I waken
Hoping for the next fix
Anticpating the terror

THUNDERBOLT

Sliding through atmosphere
Like a shark sinister
Belly pregnant with death
Armoured as a knight errant

Avenger cannon howls in fury
Her engines whine with power
Cold hard eyes search for targets
By day and night she hunts

She is a savage carnivore
Preying for the enemy to come
Shock armies tremble in fear
She is democratic death

GRASSHOPPER 1

The journey grasshopper
Of a thousand miles
Begins with, busted fan belt
And a flat tyre

GRASSHOPPER 2

Do not walk in front
I shall not follow
Do not walk behind
I shall not lead
In fact grasshopper
Keep the hell away!

PETALS

A single petal falls in silence
and
Completes the sound of darkness

INTERLUDE

Only between us
Does it matter
This one actOf love

Played out in
A beautiful garden
This place of
Our choosing

TORY

Tories live on a high chlosteral diet
Cos' they feed OFF the fat of the land

MANIC DEPRESSION

I ride the chaos winds
Again

My soul, spiralling down
Again

Turbo-charged nightmare
Again

Dragon takes me high
Again

Brain cell shuffle
Again

Head full of hell-fire
Again

"14-18, 39-45"

The French,
Have never,
Forgiven us,
For being,
Their allies.

UNREASONED BEHAVIOUR

What we fear,
We hate,

What we hate,
We fear.

EVERYTHING

To love
and
Be loved

This is
all
There is

MOOD RIDER

I ride the crest of my moods
from sunrise to sunset
and within the dark of the night

Through the darkness of my nightmares
I face the trauma of the day
till I see your face again

In the break of the dawn

GALACTIC ODYSSEY

From rim to hub
Full fifty billion lights
Passing stars, average, small, large

Pulsars spinning and skipping
Pransing like infinite ballerinas
Cross the vastness between the stars
Philosophers seek answers
Intelligence ask questions

CHOP IT OFF

They vasectimise the addicts
CHOP ITOFF

Next the beggars and outcasts
CHOP ITOFF

The the prisoners and drunks
CHOP ITOFF

Don't step on the grass, Citizen
CHOP ITOFF

Bi-polar, Schizophrenia, Depressed
CHOP ITOFF

Don't see things the way I do
CHOP ITOFF

Printed in the United States
By Bookmasters